Simple Steps For *more* Meaningful Prayer

Walnut Springs Press
110 South 800 West
Brigham City, UT
Http://walnutspringspress.blogspot.com

ISBN 978-1-93521-728-2

Portions of this book previously published in *101 Ideas for More Meaningful Prayer (Leatherwood Press, 2005)*

Simple Steps For *more* Meaningful Prayer

Leigh Brown

WALNUT SPRINGS PRESS

Introduction

It all begins and ends with prayer. Church meetings begin and end with prayer. Family home evenings begin and end with prayer. Each day of our lives should, if we heed the prophets, begin with prayer and end with prayer. We're blessed as babies and our graves are dedicated when we die. The standing joke is that if Mormons had their way, car repair would begin and end with prayer.

But there is a great principle underlying our propensity to pray. Prayer is the most fundamental expression of spirituality and the foundation for all religious experience. President David O. McKay called it the "the pulsation of a yearning, loving heart in tune with the Infinite" (David O. McKay, *Pathways to Happiness* [Salt Lake City: Deseret Book Co., 1957], 225). And echoes of its fundamental importance are quite deliberately all around us. The Book of Mormon begins and ends with prayer. It starts with the humble prayer of a prophet yearning for the righteousness of his people: "Wherefore it came to pass that my father, Lehi, as he went forth prayed unto the Lord, yea, even with all his heart, in behalf of this people. And it came to pass that as he prayed unto the Lord, there came a pillar of fire and dwelt upon a rock before him; and he saw and heard much" (1 Nephi 1:5–6). And it ends in much the same way. In the last chapter of the Book of Mormon, the prophet Moroni exhorts us to pray: "Behold, I would exhort you that when ye shall read these things, if it be wisdom in God that ye should

read them . . . that ye would ask God, the Eternal Father, in the name of Christ, if these things are not true" (Moroni 10:4).

In our own dispensation, all the glories of the Restoration quite pointedly begin with prayer: "At length I came to the conclusion that I must either remain in darkness and confusion, or else I must do as James directs, that is, ask of God. I at length came to the determination to 'ask of God,' concluding that if he gave wisdom to them that lacked wisdom, and would give liberally, and not upbraid, I might venture. So, in accordance with this, my determination to ask of God, I retired to the woods to make the attempt" (Joseph Smith—History 1:13–14).

The truth is that we cannot begin our own spiritual journey without prayer. In the second chapter of the Book of Mormon, young Nephi tells us the foundation of his own spiritual quest: "And it came to pass that I, Nephi, being exceedingly young, nevertheless being large in stature, and also having great desires to know of the mysteries of God, wherefore, I did cry unto the Lord; and behold he did visit me, and did soften my heart and I did believe in the words which have been spoken by my father" (1 Nephi 2:16).

It will begin and end with prayer for us too. And how we learn to pray—how effective our communications with Deity become from day to day—has everything to do with how things go in the middle.

President Brigham Young declared, "Were I to draw a distinction in all the duties that are required of the children of men, from first to last, I would place first and foremost the duty of seeking unto the Lord our God until we open the path of communication from heaven

to earth—from God to our own souls" (Brigham Young, *Discourses of Brigham Young,* comp. John A. Widtsoe [Salt Lake City: Deseret Book Co., 1954], 41). President Heber J. Grant taught, "Earnest, honest, and sincere prayer to God is worth more to you than all I can say or write" (Heber J. Grant, *Improvement Era,* Apr. 1938 [Salt Lake City: Deseret Book Co., 2009]). And President Gordon B. Hinckley stated that "nothing helps so much as putting a matter in the hands of the Lord. . . . Prayer is a marvelous and miraculous resource, the most marvelous and miraculous resource we have available to us" (Gordon B. Hinckley, address given 20 Apr. 1996 at Smithfield/ Logan Utah Regional Conference).

Prayer is the purest form of worship. It doesn't require a pulpit or any equipment. It doesn't take a group, although we can pray with others. It doesn't have to be done in certain places or at certain times; in fact we are commanded to "pray always" (Luke 21:36) and to "pray . . . in [our] heart" (D&C 19:28) wherever we go. Yet power in prayer is a lifetime pursuit.

This book contains dozens of ideas for more meaningful prayer. Some are practical suggestions about how, when, and where we pray. Some clarify the doctrine of prayer. The ideas are supported by scripture and by counsel from Church leaders.

The Lord wants each of us to be powerful in prayer. We hope that as you read through this collection of ideas, you will discover new ways to improve your prayers and come closer to Heaven. Ultimately, it will be the Spirit of God that will teach you to pray, but the words of scripture and inspired leaders can help point the way.

Pray Vocally

The Lord has commanded, "Thou shalt pray vocally as well as in thy heart; yea, before the world as well as in secret, in public as well as in private" (D&C 19:28). President Spencer W. Kimball reflected, "It was a prayer, a very special prayer, which opened this whole dispensation! It began with a young man's first vocal prayer. I hope that not too many of our prayers are silent" (Spencer W. Kimball, "We Need a Listening Ear," *Ensign*, Nov. 1979, 4). Praying out loud helps us visualize the humble process of petitioning our Father in Heaven. We are also better able to focus on the words of our prayer and are less easily distracted by diverting thoughts.

Accompany Prayer with Scripture Study

Our prayers will improve when offered in accordance with studying and understanding the scriptures. President Ezra Taft Benson promised, "When individual members and families immerse themselves in the scriptures regularly and consistently . . . personal revelation will flow" (Ezra Taft Benson, "The Power of the Word," *Ensign,* May 1986, 80). Elder Bruce R. McConkie testified of the importance of scripture study in receiving personal revelation: "I sometimes think that one of the best-kept secrets of the kingdom is that the scriptures open the door to the receipt of revelation. . . . The prayerful study and pondering of the holy scriptures will do as much, or more than any other single thing, to bring that spirit, the spirit of prophecy and the spirit of revelation, into our lives" (Bruce R. McConkie, *Sermons and Writings of Bruce R. McConkie* [Salt Lake City: Deseret Book Co., 1989], 243–44). If we are truly seeking personal revelation in our prayers, scripture study must be cherished as a key to opening the heavens.

Wait and Listen for a Few Minutes after Praying

Elder Neal A. Maxwell said, "We are often not only too slow to get on our knees but too quick to rise from them, as if prayer involved physical calisthenics" (Neal A. Maxwell, *Deposition of a Disciple* [Salt Lake City: Deseret Book Co., 1976], 19). If we wait patiently after we have concluded our prayer, we open the door for further revelation. President Spencer W. Kimball taught, "Sometimes ideas flood our mind as we listen after our prayers. Sometimes feelings press upon us. A spirit of calmness assures us that all will be well. But always, if we have been honest and earnest [in our prayers] we will experience a good feeling—a feeling of warmth for our Father in Heaven and a sense of his love for us" (Spencer W. Kimball, "Pray Always," *Ensign,* Oct. 1981, 3). Waiting patiently and attentively after prayer is a small sacrifice to make for the revelation the Lord promises to grant us.

Believe That Heavenly Father Is Listening

In counsel to Hezekiah, the prophet Isaiah stated: "Thus saith the Lord God of Israel, That which thou hast prayed to me . . . I have heard" (2 Kings 19:20). The Lord does hear our prayers. And the more we believe that He does, the more powerful our prayers become. Joseph F. Smith recounted his feelings about Heber C. Kimball's manner of prayer: "I was greatly impressed and moved by his manner of praying in his family. I have never heard any other man pray as he did. He did not speak to the Lord as one afar off, but as if conversing with him face to face. Time and again I have been so impressed with the idea of the actual presence of God, while he was conversing with him in prayer, that I could not refrain from looking up to see if he were actually present and visible" (Joseph F. Smith, *Gospel Doctrine,* comp. John A. Widtsoe [Salt Lake City: Deseret Book Co., 1919], 197). Such intimate prayer is powerful prayer.

Pray for Those in Need

President Gordon B. Hinckley said, "What a wonderful thing it is to remember before the Lord those who are sick and in sorrow, those who are hungry and destitute, those who are lonely and afraid, those who are in bondage and sore distress. When such prayers are uttered in sincerity, there will follow a greater desire to reach out to those in need" (Gordon B. Hinckley, *Faith: The Essence of True Religion* [Salt Lake City: Deseret Book Co., 1971], 71). Praying for others helps us become more like our Heavenly Father and our Savior as we learn to embody Christlike love and service. Sincere prayer on behalf of others can soften our hearts and invoke the Lord's tenderness towards our own supplications. The Prophet Joseph Smith taught, "The nearer we get to our heavenly Father, the more we are disposed to look with compassion on perishing souls; we feel that we want to take them upon our shoulders, and cast their sins behind our backs. . . . If you would have God have mercy on you, have mercy on one another" (Smith, *Teachings,* 241).

Sing a Hymn before Praying

The words of the hymns are considered scripture and can help to prepare our minds and hearts to address our Heavenly Father. The Lord has assured, "For my soul delighteth in the song of the heart; yea, the song of the righteous is a prayer unto me, and it shall be answered with a blessing upon their heads" (D&C 25:12). Hymns call forth a spirit of humility and reverence that can help us become ready to hear and understand the mind and will of God. It is a regular practice in most Church meetings to sing a hymn before addressing our Heavenly Father in prayer. And we can emulate that same preparation in our private or family prayers. The hymns of Zion will bring a spirit of reverence and focus to our prayers. Singing hymns can be a manifestation of our willingness to be humble and will call down blessings upon our heads.

Doubt Not and Fear Not

Feelings of doubt and fear can cast out faith, which is essential to effective prayer. Joseph Smith taught, "Doubt and faith do not reside in the same person at the same time" (Joseph Smith, *Lectures on Faith* [Salt Lake City: Deseret Book Co., 1835], 6:12). To ensure a powerful prayer, we must root out any doubt before we pray. Elder Gene R. Cook said, "One of the greatest difficulties of trying to accomplish something through faith and prayer is to really believe it will happen. Doubt and fear are so powerful that they can sometimes dissuade you from starting the endeavor in the first place, or when you get started they can motivate you to quit" (Cook, *Answers*, 54–55). Doubt can hinder our righteous desires. "When we worry about the future," Elder Joseph B. Wirthlin explained, "we create unhappiness in the present. Righteous concern may lead us to take appropriate action, but worrying about things we cannot control can paralyze and demoralize us" (Joseph B. Wirthlin, "Improving Our Prayers," *Ensign*, Mar. 2004, 24).

Pray Together as a Family, Both Morning and Night

The Savior commanded, "Pray in your families unto the Father, always in my name, that your wives and your children may be blessed" (3 Nephi 18:21). When family members pray together, they develop a more Christlike love in the home and begin to see one another as God does. Through praying together, family members learn more about each other's hopes and concerns and are better able to help and take care of each other. "The holding of family prayer is a powerful influence for good in every home where it is a regular practice," Elder Franklin D. Richards stated. "Morning and evening prayers, as well as the blessing on our food, bring us a sense of unity in our family as well as a closeness to our Father in heaven." (Franklin D. Richards, "The Importance of Prayer," *Ensign,* July 1973, 66). President Spencer W. Kimball taught, "The Church urges that there be family prayer every night and every morning. It is a kneeling prayer with all or as many members of the family present as possible. Many have found the most effective time is at the breakfast and at the dinner table. These prayers need not be long, especially if little children are on their knees. All of the members of the family, including the little ones, should have opportunity to be mouth in the prayer, in turn" (Spencer W. Kimball, *Faith Precedes the Miracle* [Salt Lake City: Deseret Book Co., 1972], 200).

Pray to Strengthen Your Testimony

Elder Reed Smoot taught, "It is so vital to a man and woman, no matter what position they hold, in order that they may maintain a testimony, if they have one, of the Gospel of Jesus Christ; and if they haven't yet that testimony, I know of no better way in all the world to receive it than to plead with our Heavenly Father that it may be granted unto them" (Reed Smoot, *Conference Report,* Oct. 1932 [Salt Lake City: Deseret Book Co., 2009], 85). While a testimony can increase or decrease daily, prayer is the power we can use to keep it growing. President Harold B. Lee cautioned, "The testimony we have to day will not be our testimony of tomorrow. Our testimony is either going to grow and grow until it becomes as the brightness of the sun, or it is going to diminish to nothing, depending on what we do about it." Prayer is essential for conversion to the gospel of Christ. And praying for a strengthened testimony prepares us for future challenges. "To meet the difficulties that are coming," President Heber C. Kimball warned, "it will be necessary for you to have a knowledge of the truth of this work for yourselves. . . . The time will come when no man nor woman will be able to endure on borrowed light. Each will have to be guided by the light within himself" (quoted in Orson F. Whitney, *The Life of Heber C. Kimball* [Salt Lake City: Deseret Book Co., 1888], 450).

Strive to Better Understand the Character of God

The Prophet Joseph Smith observed that "it is the first principle of the gospel to know for a certainty the character of God, and to know that we may converse with Him as one man converses with another" (Joseph Smith, *Teachings of the Prophet Joseph Smith,* comp. Joseph Fielding Smith [Salt Lake City: Deseret Book Co., 1938], 345). Improving our understanding of the character of God is not only important, but it is necessary for more meaningful prayer. As emphasized by Elder Bernard P. Brockbank, "To pray meaningfully requires that one, insofar as possible, knows the true character of God . . . we have been commanded to know God. Prayer leads to salvation, and ignorance is a deterrent to that goal" (Bernard P. Brockbank, "Prayer to Our Heavenly Father," *Ensign,* Nov. 1979, 58). To learn the character of God we must study the scriptures. Joseph Smith emphasized the importance of searching God's word to better understand His character: "As we have been indebted to a revelation which God made of himself to his creatures, in the first instance, for the idea of his existence, so in like manner we are indebted to the revelations which he has given to us for a correct understanding of his character, perfections, and attributes; because without the revelations which he has given to us, no man by searching could find out God" (Smith, *Lectures,* 3:7). But prayer

itself can be a means to coming to know God. Charles W. Penrose taught how prayer is necessary to better comprehend the character of God: "No man by his own researches can find out God. He may, by reason and reflection, by observing and pondering upon the wonders of creation, by studying his own internal and external nature, come to the sure conclusion that there is a God, and to a very small extent make an estimate of his character. But without the Almighty manifests Himself in some manner, finite man can never obtain a knowledge of infinite Deity" (Charles W. Penrose, *Contributor,* vol. 2 [Oct. 1880–Sept. 1881], no. 1 [Salt Lake City: Deseret Book Co., 2009], 7).

Ask for Truth

As part of our prayers, we should ask for the light and inspiration the Lord desires to give us. The Lord taught, "Ask, and ye shall receive; knock, and it shall be opened unto you" (D&C 4:7). President Joseph Fielding Smith stated, "There is no reason in the world why any soul should not know where to find the truth. If he will only humble himself and seek in the spirit of humility and faith, going to the Lord just as the Prophet Joseph Smith went to the Lord to find the truth, he will find it. There's no doubt about it" (Smith, *Salvation,* 1:293). We can be privileged to receive truth, but we must ask for it and seek the Spirit that confirms it. "Behold, thou knowest that thou hast inquired of me and I did enlighten thy mind; and now I tell thee these things that thou mayest know that thou hast been enlightened by the Spirit of truth" (D&C 6:15). Marion G. Romney emphasized that prayer is the only way to find truth: "The spirit of revelation turns the key which opens the mind and spirit of man to an understanding of the gospel. There is no other key to such knowledge. Thinkers have philosophized; poets have dreamed, and scientists have experimented, but only God speaks with a sure knowledge of all truth" (Marion G. Romney, *Look to God and Live* [Salt Lake City: Deseret Book Co., 1971], 65).

Pray to Discover Heavenly Father's Will for You

Elder Neal A. Maxwell noted, "So very much of pure prayer seems to be the process of first discovering, rather than requesting, the will of our Father in heaven and then aligning ourselves therewith" (Neal A. Maxwell, *All These Things Shall Give Thee Experience* [Salt Lake City: Deseret Book Co., 1979], 93). We must listen closely during our prayers as we seek to know what our Father desires for us. The Lord has promised to reveal His will to those who hearken to His Spirit: "For by my Spirit will I enlighten them, and by my power will I make known unto them the secrets of my will" (D&C 76:10). The Bible Dictionary states, "Prayer is the act by which the will of the Father and the will of the child are brought into correspondence with each other. The object of prayer is not to change the will of God, but to secure for ourselves and for others blessings that God is already willing to grant, but that are made conditional on our asking for them" (Bible Dictionary, "Prayer," 752–53). Ultimately, it is our choice to follow either God's will or our own. As Elder Rex D. Pinegar said, "If we, like the Savior, have the faith to put our trust in our Father in Heaven, to submit to his will, the true spirit of peace will come as a witness and strength that he has heard and answered our prayers" ("Miracle of Prayer: God Hears, Answers," *LDS Church News,* 10 Apr. 1993 [Salt Lake City: Deseret Book Co., 2009],18).

Kneel to Pray

The Lord has commanded us to kneel in prayer: "Let him offer himself in prayer upon his knees before God, in token or remembrance of the everlasting covenant" (D&C 88:131). This one simple act helps us remember our position before God, and we can better reverence Him as we humble ourselves in His presence. President Gordon B. Hinckley explained, "There is something in the very posture of kneeling that contradicts the attitudes described by Paul; 'proud . . . heady, highminded'" (Gordon B. Hinckley, *Be Thou an Example* [Salt Lake City: Deseret Book Co., 1981], 31). Assuming the physical posture of humility can help prepare us to listen and receive the Lord's direction in prayer.

Acknowledge That You Need the Lord's Help

While we sometimes long to be independent, we must recognize that we ultimately need to rely on God in order to make it successfully through life. President Gordon B. Hinckley emphasized, "You can't do it alone. You know that. You cannot make it alone and do your best. You need the help of the Lord . . . and the marvelous thing is that you have the opportunity to pray, with the expectation that your prayers will be heard and answered" (Gordon B. Hinckley, *Teachings of Gordon B. Hinckley* [Salt Lake City: Deseret Book Co., 1997], 468). "No person possesses intelligence, in any degree," noted Brigham Young, "that he has not received from the God of heaven, or, in other words, from the Fountain of all intelligence, whether he acknowledges his God in it or not. No man, independent of the Great Ruler of the universe, is capable of devising that which we see and are well acquainted with. All mechanism, good government, wholesome principle, and true philosophy of whatever name or nature, flows from God to finite man" (Young, *Discourses*, 148). Acknowledging our dependence on our Father in Heaven is a way for us to develop a humble and contrite heart as we petition for His love and support.

Pray to Know Your Standing before God

At an early age, Joseph Smith understood the importance of this principle. He recorded the feelings he had at age seventeen: "I often felt condemned for my weakness and imperfections; when . . . I betook myself to prayer and supplication to Almighty God for forgiveness of all my sins and follies, and also for a manifestation to me, that I might know of my state and standing before him; for I had full confidence in obtaining a divine manifestation" (Joseph Smith—History 1:29). Praying to know our weaknesses and imperfections is a necessary step in becoming clean and obtaining salvation. President John Taylor declared, "I know . . . we have our trials, afflictions, sorrows, and privations; we meet with difficulties; we have to contend with the world, with the powers of darkness, with the corruptions of men, and a variety of evils; yet at the same time through these things we have to be made perfect. It is necessary that we should have a knowledge of ourselves, of our true position and standing before God, and comprehend our strength, our weakness, our ignorance and intelligence, our wisdom and our folly, that we may know how to appreciate true principles, and comprehend, and put a proper value upon, all things as they present themselves before our minds. It is necessary that we should know our own weaknesses and the weaknesses of our fellowmen; our own strength, as well as

the strength of others; and comprehend our true position before God, angels, and men; that we may be inclined to treat all with due respect, and not to over-value our own wisdom or strength, nor depreciate it, or that of others, but put our trust in the living God, and follow after Him" (John Taylor, in *Journal of Discourses*, 26 vols. [Salt Lake City: Deseret Book Co., 2009], 1:148). Like the Prophet Joseph, we can approach our Maker with confidence that He will reveal our standing before Him so we might know where to seek improvement.

Be Honest with Heavenly Father and Yourself

Moroni cautioned that it is "counted evil unto a man, if he shall pray and not with real intent of heart; yea, and it profiteth him nothing, for God receiveth none such" (Moroni 7:9). The Lord knows our hearts, and He will bless us according to our straightforward pleadings. When we are open with our Heavenly Father and express our honest feelings and concerns to Him, we simultaneously come to understand more about our true selves. Elder Neal A. Maxwell noted that "we cannot, for the purposes of real prayer, hurriedly dress our words and attitudes in tuxedos when our shabby life is in rags. More than we realize, being honest with God in our prayers helps us to be more honest with ourselves" (Maxwell, *Experience,* 93).

Keep Practicing

No one prays perfectly all the time. Perhaps one reason we are commanded to pray so frequently is that, as with everything else, we will become better with practice. Elder Neal A. Maxwell taught that "given the times in which we live, improving our prayers should be one of our deepest desires if we are genuinely serious about growing spiritually" (Maxwell, *Experience*, 91). Later, he stated, "Neither the pure City of Enoch nor pure prayers are arrived at in a day!" (Ibid, 95). Meaningful prayer takes time and effort. We improve through practice and should continually strive to make each prayer worthy of the divine Creator whom we are addressing. Elder H. Burke Peterson taught, "To learn to communicate with [God], to learn to pray effectively, requires diligence and dedication and desire on our part" (H. Burke Peterson, "Adversity and Prayer," in *Prayer,* compilation [Salt Lake City: Deseret Book Co., 1977], 108).

Follow the Lord's Counsel to Seek Further Revelation

The Lord promises to give us further revelation once we have heeded the revelation that He has already given. In 2 Nephi 28:30, "I will give unto the children of men line upon line, precept upon precept, here a little and there a little; and blessed are those who hearken unto my precepts, and lend an ear unto my counsel, for they shall learn wisdom; for unto him that receiveth I will give more; and from them that shall say, We have enough, from them shall be taken away even that which they have" (2 Nephi 28:30). We cannot expect to receive more revelation, President Joseph Fielding Smith counseled, unless we follow what we have: "Revelation is promised us through our faithfulness. . . . The Lord withholds much that he would otherwise reveal if the members of the Church were prepared to receive it. . . . We have little occasion to clamor for more revelation when we refuse to heed what the Lord has revealed for our salvation" (Joseph Fielding Smith, *Doctrines of Salvation,* 3 vols., ed. Bruce R. McConkie [Salt Lake City: Deseret Book Co., 1954], 1:283). Likewise, we are blessed according to our diligence: "It is given unto many to know the mysteries of God; nevertheless they are laid under a strict command that they shall not impart only according to the portion of his word which he doth grant unto the children of men, according to the heed and diligence which

they give unto him" (Alma 12:9). And according to our courage, as President Joseph F. Smith taught: "And when we live so that we can hear and understand the whisperings of the still small voice of the Spirit of God, let us do whatsoever that Spirit directs, without fear of the consequences. . . let us do it, no matter what men may say or think" (Joseph F. Smith, *Conference Report,* Oct. 1903 [Salt Lake City: Deseret Book Co., 2009], 97).

Pray in a Quiet Place

Praying in a quiet place allows us to concentrate on our communication with our Heavenly Father. Background noise easily distracts our attention when we need to focus on our supplication to God and on His responses to us. Jesus Christ was an example of this as He sought a quiet private place to pray. Luke records: "And he came out, and went, as he was wont, to the mount of Olives; and his disciples also followed him. . . . And he was withdrawn from them about a stone's cast, and kneeled down, and prayed" (Luke 22:39, 41). When you pray, separate yourselves from the rest of the world and let your mind and heart focus on the things of God.

Be Humble

"Be thou humble; and the Lord thy God shall lead thee by the hand, and give thee answer to thy prayers" (D&C 112:10). Through humility, our hearts are more open to the Lord and His will for us. "The principle of humility and prayer," said President David O. McKay, "leads one to feel a need of divine guidance. Self-reliance is a virtue, but with it should go a consciousness of the need of superior help—a consciousness that as you walk firmly in the pathway of duty, there is a possibility of your making a misstep; and with that consciousness is a prayer, a pleading that God will inspire you to avoid that false step" (McKay, *Happiness,* 226). The Lord promises personal revelation to the humble: "I speak unto you . . . concerning the man that desires the witness—Behold, I say unto him, he exalts himself and does not humble himself sufficiently before me; but if he will bow down before me, and humble himself in mighty prayer and faith, in the sincerity of his heart, then will I grant unto him a view of the things which he desires to see" (D&C 5:23–24). President Gordon B. Hinckley said, "The meek and the humble are those who are teachable. They are willing to learn. They are willing to listen to the whisperings of the still, small voice for guidance in their lives." (Gordon B. Hinckley, "A Prophet's Counsel and Prayer for Youth," *Ensign,* Jan. 2001, 2).

Pray to Recognize and Acknowledge the Lord's Hand in Your Life

"And in nothing doth man offend God, or against none is his wrath kindled, save those who confess not his hand in all things, and obey not his commandments" (D&C 59:21). Acknowledging God's hand means not only taking note of the blessings He has granted us, but also recognizing His awareness of and participation in much that unfolds in our lives. The psalmist declared, "O give thanks unto the Lord; call upon his name: make known his deeds among the people" (Psalms 105:1). If we pray for protection every morning, for example, we should acknowledge in our evening prayers the mercy of the Lord in His preservation of us that day. King Benjamin reminds us that the Lord "is preserving you from day to day, by lending you breath, that ye may live and move and do according to your own will, and even supporting you from one moment to another" (Mosiah 2:21). When we note that God made it possible for certain things to happen or *not* to happen during our day, we demonstrate our faith in Him. Recognizing God's hand in our lives also leads us to recommit to living as He would have us live.

Ask Heavenly Father to Manifest His Love for You

"One of the greatest daily evidences we have of God's great love for each of us," Elder Marvin J. Ashton declared, "is our relationship to Him in our prayers" (Marvin J. Ashton, *Ye Are My Friends* [Salt Lake City: Deseret Book Co., 1972], 36). Our Heavenly Father loves us beyond measure and desires to express His love to us. When we ask Him with humility for a manifestation of this love, we can receive a powerful witness. "When filled with God's love," Elder John H. Groberg testified, "we can do and see and understand things that we could not otherwise do or see or understand. Filled with his love, we can endure pain, quell fear, forgive freely, avoid contention, renew strength, and bless and help others in ways surprising even to us" (John H. Groberg, "The Power of God's Love," *Ensign*, Nov. 2004, 9).

Pray for Strength through Trials and Chastisement

Often, our trials are not meant to be removed but to be endured, for our own growth and benefit. Elder Richard L. Evans proclaimed, "Most of us might be disposed to pray for unbroken good fortune, for uninterrupted happiness, for perpetual prosperity, for victory, for assured success, for affluence and ease. But life isn't an uninterrupted holiday; nor, obviously, was it intended to be. Rather it is a time of training, and often of trial, of education, and of self-effort, . . . Prayer is not a matter of asking only. It should not be always as the beggar's upturned hand. Often the purpose of prayer is to give us strength to do what needs to be done, wisdom to see the way to solve our own problems, and ability to do our best in our tasks. We need to pray not only for freedom from difficulty but for strength to endure, for faith and fortitude to face what sometimes must be faced" (Richard L. Evans, *The Man and the Message* [Salt Lake City: Deseret Book, 1973], 289). Following counsel and chastisement from the Lord also requires more strength in order for us to move forward and progress through our difficulties. As Brigham Young taught, "I know it is hard to receive chastisement, for no chastisement is joyous, but grievous at the time it is given; but if a person will receive chastisement and pray for the Holy Spirit to rest upon him, that he may have the Spirit of truth in

---

his heart, and cleave to that which is pleasing to the Lord, the Lord will give him grace to bear the chastisement, and he will submit to and receive it, knowing that it is for his good" (Brigham Young in *Journal of Discourses,* [Salt Lake City: Deseret Book Co., 2009], 3:47).

Let Your Prayers Come from the Heart

Sometimes when we pray, we say the words but our heart is not involved and our mind is not focused. The Lord Himself declared, "And ye shall seek me, and find me, when ye shall search for me with all your heart" (Jeremiah 29:13). President Joseph F. Smith taught, "True, faithful, earnest prayer consists more in the feeling that rises from the heart and from the inward desire of our spirits to supplicate the Lord in humility and in faith, that we may receive his blessings. It matters not how simple the words may be, if our desires are genuine and we come before the Lord with a broken heart and contrite spirit to ask him for that which we need" (Joseph F. Smith, *Conference Report,* Apr. 1935 [Salt Lake City: Deseret Book Co., 1935]). Praying from the heart means that we send a bit of our souls heavenward. President David O. McKay instructed, "Prayer is the pulsation of a yearning, loving heart in tune with the Infinite. It is a message of the soul sent directly to a loving Father. The language is not mere words" (David O. McKay, *Treasures of Life*, comp. Clare Middlemiss [Salt Lake City: Deseret Book Co.,1962], 308).

Pray with Greater Desire

"If we want something for this Church and Kingdom, or if we want something for our individual lives," said Elder John A. Widtsoe, "we must have a great, earnest, overpowering desire for that thing. We must reach out for it, with full faith in our Heavenly Father that the gift may be given us. Then it would seem as if the Lord himself cannot resist our petition. If our desire is strong enough, if our whole will is tempered and attuned to that which we desire, if our lives make us worthy of the desired gift, the Lord, by his own words, is bound to give us that which we desire, in his own time and in his own manner" (John A. Widtsoe, *Conference Report,* Apr. 1935 [Salt Lake City: Deseret Book Co., 2009], 82). Greater power accompanies greater desire in prayer. "The effectual fervent prayer of a righteous man availeth much" (James 5:16). We can always pray with greater desire, and the Lord will bless us with this desire as we seek it. For example, after the Lord's visitation, the Nephites prayed earnestly and "they did not multiply many words, for it was given unto them what they should pray, and they were filled with desire" (3 Nephi 19:24). "As we prepare our minds and hearts for prayer," Elder Gene R. Cook taught, "we can increase our desire to talk to the Lord, we can seek more fully to align our desires with those of God, and we can desire more fully to receive answers from him" (Cook, *Answers,* 26).

Keep a Prayer in Your Heart

President Joseph F. Smith taught, "We should carry with us the spirit of prayer throughout every duty that we have to perform in life. Why should we? One of the simple reasons that appeals to my mind with great force is that man is so utterly dependent upon God! How helpless we are without him; how little can we do without his merciful providence in our behalf!" (Joseph F. Smith, *Conference Report,* Oct. 1914 [Salt Lake City: Deseret Book Co.], 6). With a prayer in our hearts, we have continuous access to a Higher Power. Elder Marvin J. Ashton emphasized the importance of this blessing: "We have been commanded to pray under all conditions wherever we are. Our spirits are heaven-drawn, anxious for constant communication with the source of all great strength" (Marvin J. Ashton, "Personal Prayers," in *Prayer,* 7). The prophet Amulek testified, "When you do not cry unto the Lord, let your hearts be full, drawn out in prayer unto him continually for your welfare, and also for the welfare of those who are around you" (Alma 34:27). Praying in our hearts while we go about our daily routines is a commandment that blesses our lives and the lives around us.

Pray in Faith

God's power follows prayers of faith. The power of Alma's great faith called forth an angel of God to chastise his wayward son: "And again, the angel said: Behold, the Lord hath heard the prayers of his people, and also the prayers of his servant, Alma, who is thy father; for he has prayed with much faith concerning thee that thou mightest be brought to the knowledge of the truth; therefore, for this purpose have I come to convince thee of the power and authority of God, that the prayers of his servants might be answered according to their faith" (Mosiah 27:14). Personal revelation follows prayers of faith. As the Prophet Joseph Smith succinctly stated, "The only way to obtain truth and wisdom, is not to ask it from books, but to go to God in prayer and obtain divine teaching" (Joseph Smith, *The Words of Joseph Smith*, ed. Andrew F. Ehat and Lyndon W. Cook [Provo, UT: BYU Religious Studies Center, 1980], 77.)

Forget the Cares of the World during Prayer

Worldly concerns can become a barrier between a petitioner and Heavenly Father. Release anxious thoughts during your prayer and let your mind become clear to receive spiritual inspiration. Paraphrasing President David O. McKay, Harold B. Lee said, "It's a great thing to be responsive to the whisperings of the Spirit, and we know that when these whisperings come it is a gift and our privilege to have them. They come when we are relaxed and not under pressure of appointment" (Harold B. Lee, *The Teachings of Harold B. Lee* [Salt Lake City: Deseret Book Co., 1996], 415). Then President Lee explained, "If we are worried about something and upset in our feelings, the inspiration does not come. If we so live that our minds are free from worry and our conscience is clear and our feelings are right toward one another, the operation of the Spirit of the Lord upon our spirit is as real as when we pick up the telephone" (Ibid). Let us follow the counsel of a beloved hymn: "There is an hour of peace and rest, unmarred by earthly care; 'tis when before the Lord I go, and kneel in secret prayer" ("Secret Prayer," *Hymns,* no. 144).

Recall Heavenly Father's Answers to You in the Past

President David O. McKay recalled powerful responses from the Lord to his humble petitions: "These experiences are part of my very being and must remain so long as memory and intelligence last" (David O. McKay, *Conference Report,* Apr. 1969 [Salt Lake City: Deseret Book Co., 2009], 153). Moments of personal revelation are sacred and should be recalled often to help us retain and strengthen our testimony of God's love for us. As we treasure up in remembrance God's answers to our prayers, our faith in prayer is increased and our prayers become more powerful. In the Book of Mormon, Alma asks if we have "sufficiently retained in remembrance" the Lord's blessings and if we can still feel in our hearts to "sing the song of redeeming love" (Alma 5:6, 26). In 1829, the Lord commanded Oliver Cowdery to remember important answers that he had received from prayer: "Behold, thou knowest that thou hast inquired of me and I did enlighten thy mind . . . if you desire a further witness, cast your mind upon the night that you cried unto me in your heart. . . . Did I not speak peace to your mind concerning the matter? What greater witness can you have than from God?" (D&C 6:15, 22–23).

Be Reverent during Your Prayers

President David O. McKay taught, "[An] essential virtue [in effective prayer] is reverence. This virtue is exemplified in the model prayer given by the Savior in the words 'Hallowed by thy name.' This principle should be exemplified in classrooms, and particularly in our houses of worship" (McKay, *Happiness,* 226). Revering God requires that we focus our hearts and our minds on Him, and that we approach Him with respect and awe. Elder Bruce R. McConkie counseled: "Our Father is glorified and exalted; he is an omnipotent being. We are as the dust of the earth in comparison, and yet we are his children with access, through prayer, to his presence. . . . We approach Deity in the spirit of awe, reverence, and worship. We speak in hushed and solemn tones. . . . We are at our best in prayer" (Bruce R. McConkie, "Why the Lord Ordained Prayer," *Ensign,* Jan. 1976, 7).

Pray for Civic Leaders

The Apostle Paul instructed, "I exhort therefore, that, first of all, supplications, prayers, intercessions, and giving of thanks, be made for all men; For kings, and for all that are in authority; that we may lead a quiet and peaceable life in all godliness and honesty. For this is good and acceptable in the sight of God our Saviour; Who will have all men to be saved, and to come unto the knowledge of the truth" (1 Timothy 2:1–4). Likewise, President Ezra Taft Benson taught, "Pray in your homes morning and evening. Pray for civil magistrates and leaders even when you do not agree with them. . . . Pray, as you have been counseled, that the doors of nations of the world will be opened to the preaching of the gospel" (Ezra Taft Benson, "May the Kingdom of God Go Forth," *Ensign,* May 1978, 20). As we pray for leaders of the world to guide their people in a way conducive to building the kingdom of God, we come to care more for the people of the world and for the spreading of the gospel across the earth. Our petitions are needed for the furthering of the Lord's work.

Improve Your Relationship with Heavenly Father

Your relationship with your Heavenly Father will expand as you strive to keep His commandments and follow the promptings of His Spirit. While serving in the Quorum of the Twelve Apostles, David O. McKay declared, "I feel as I have never felt before in all my life that God is my Father. His is not just an intangible power, a moral force in the world, but a personal God with creative power, the Governor of the world, the Director of our souls. I would have [people] feel so close to Him that they will approach Him daily, not in public alone, but in private" (David O. McKay, *Conference Report,* Apr. 1922 [Salt Lake City: Deseret Book Co., 2009], 64). Brigham Young also testified of the importance of feeling close to our Father in Heaven: "When you approach the throne of grace and petition the Father, in the name of the Savior who has redeemed the world, do you use the name as the name of a stranger? If you understand your own religion, you petition that Personage as you would one of your brethren in the flesh. Is this strange to you? It should bring near to you things that pertain to eternity, give your reflections and views a more exalted cast, stamp your daily actions with truth and honesty, and cause you to be, filled with the Spirit and power of God" (Young, *Discourses,* 43). Our feelings toward God are based on worship and awe, making

this relationship unlike any earthly relationship, yet two-way communication is just as critical. As we grow in commitment and affection for our Heavenly Father, our prayers will be a natural outgrowth of our desire to be near Him.

Continually Pray for Guidance

The prophet Nephi taught, "I say unto you that ye must pray always, and not faint; that ye must not perform any thing unto the Lord save in the first place ye shall pray unto the Father, in the name of Christ, that he will consecrate thy performance unto thee, that thy performance may be for the welfare of thy soul" (2 Nephi 32:9). It is important that we pray for God's direction in not only major life decisions, but in all aspects of daily life. President Heber J. Grant warned that "the minute a man stops supplicating God for his spirit and directions just so soon he starts out to become a stranger to him and his works. When men stop praying for God's spirit, they place confidence in their own unaided reason, and they gradually lose the spirit of God, just the same as near and dear friends, by never writing to or visiting with each other, will become strangers" (Heber J. Grant, *Conference Report,* Oct. 1944 [Salt Lake City: Deseret Book Co., 2009], 9). While the ups and downs of life may lead us to slacken or rededicate our efforts in our earthly work, we must never allow ourselves to become lax in our daily devotions to God.

Prepare Your Thoughts before You Pray

Because our lives are full and our days busy, preparation for prayer is critical. Patricia T. Holland suggested, "Find a private place and kneel comfortably and calmly in the center of the room. For a few moments say nothing, just think of him. Just kneel there and feel the closeness of his presence, his warmth, his peace" (Jeffrey R. Holland, Patricia T. Holland, *On Earth as It Is in Heaven* [Salt Lake City: Deseret Book Co., 1989], 37). Though you may not be able to remove yourself physically from the world, preparing your mind before prayer will lead to a more satisfying spiritual experience. After all, prayer is a form of work that uses your spiritual faculties.

Pray Even When You Don't Want To

Prayer is essential and should be incorporated into our daily lives regardless of our changing temperaments or attitudes. Ezra Taft Benson counseled, "If we don't feel like praying, then we should pray until we do feel like praying" (Ezra Taft Benson, *God Family, Country: Our Three Great Loyalties* [Salt Lake City: Deseret Book Co., 1974], 121). Regular, frequent prayer is a strict commandment of God. To Adam and Eve, He declared "Thou shalt repent and call upon God in the name of the Son forevermore" (Moses 5:8). Brigham Young stated: "It is your duty to pray; and when the time for prayer comes, John should say, 'This is the place and this is the time to pray: knees bend down upon that floor, and do so at once.' But John said, 'I do not want to pray; I do not feel like it.' Knees, get down, I say; and down bend the knees, and he begins to think and reflect. Can you say anything? Can you not say, God have mercy on me a sinner? Yes, he can do this . . . Now, John, open your mouth and say, Lord, have mercy upon me. 'But I do not feel the spirit of prayer.' That does not excuse you, for you know what your duty is" (Young, *Discourses*, 45).

Thank before Asking

President David O. McKay explained, "The young man who closes the door behind him, who draws the curtains, and there in silence pleads with God for help, should first pour out his soul in gratitude for health, for friends, for loved ones, for the gospel, for the manifestations of God's existence" (McKay, *Happiness,* 228–39). Expressing gratitude to the Lord before pouring out our desires and concerns not only helps prepare our souls to receive inspiration, but can change the way we perceive our needs. Sister Dwan J. Young taught, "Most of the time we think of prayer only when we want something; but when we start by expressing gratitude for the things we already have, we begin to see our lives in a new way" (Dwan J. Young, "Draw Near to Him in Prayer," *Ensign,* Nov. 1985, 91).

Know That the Lord is Always There

"But when they in their trouble did turn unto the Lord God of Israel, and sought him, he was found of them" (2 Chronicles 15:4). God has blessed us with unlimited access to Him through prayer. President James E. Faust taught, "Access to our Creator through our Savior is surely one of the great privileges and blessings of our lives. . . . There is no limit on the number of times or how long we can pray each day. There is no quota of how many needs we wish to pray for in each prayer. He is reachable at any time and any place" (James E. Faust, "The Lifeline of Prayer," *Ensign,* July 2002, 67–69). Know that whenever you need your Father in Heaven, you can pray and He is there. At the end of the book of Matthew the Lord promises, "Lo, I am with you always, even unto the end of the world" (Matthew 28:20). Since we have been baptized and received the gift of the Holy Ghost, we have special assurance that we can receive guidance and direction whenever we need it. We should have confidence that the Lord will be there for us, and we should call upon Him frequently.

Be Specific

We need to be specific in our prayers—pray for people by name, ask for specific blessings, and make specific promises to our Heavenly Father. Elder Gene R. Cook declared, "The Lord will be involved in the *specifics* of your life if you invite him to be . . . I bear testimony that the problem with most of us is that we do not ask specifically enough or perhaps with the strength of real intent. How much the Lord wants to bless us, and yet many of us will not ask" (Cook, *Answers,* 54). Concerning prayers of repentance and forgiveness, Elder Neal A. Maxwell cautioned, "A vague prayer is hardly a prayer at all. . . . We may be too embarrassed to bring before the Lord specific weaknesses we have, yet he knows of them anyway. We thus prevent ourselves from gathering and gaining the strength we might need to overcome them. Admitting aloud (though in private) our weaknesses and stating our promises is sometimes better than just thinking of them. Dealing with our specific weaknesses is far better than simply praying that we will be more righteous" (Maxwell, "What Should We Pray For?" in *Prayer,* 50–51).

Understand That Receiving Answers Will Not Always be Easy

When we petition the Lord for an answer, we should not automatically expect an immediate response. As a general rule, we must prove ourselves to the Lord before He can bless us, and this can take time and effort. "Blessings require some work or effort on our part before we can obtain them. Prayer is a form of work, and is an appointed means for obtaining the highest of all blessings" (Bible Dictionary, "Prayer," 753). Often, we must work hard to receive revelation from the Lord. Elder Bruce R. McConkie stated, "It is not, never has been, and never will be the design and purpose of the Lord—however much we seek him in prayer—to answer all our problems and concerns without struggle and effort on our part. This mortality is a probationary estate. In it we have our agency. We are being tested to see how we will respond in various situations; how we will decide issues; what course we will pursue while we are here walking, not by sight, but by faith. Hence, we are to solve our own problems and then to counsel with the Lord in prayer and receive a spiritual confirmation that our decisions are correct" (McConkie, "Why the Lord Ordained Prayer").

Sanctify Yourself before Prayer

President George Albert Smith taught, "We should know that our prayers will not avail us much unless we repent of our sins. Faith, repentance, baptism by immersion for the remission of sins, laying on of hands for the gift of the Holy Ghost, are the fundamental teachings of our Heavenly Father to us, and have been the groundwork of the Church since it was organized" (George Albert Smith, *Conference Report,* Oct. 1944 [Salt Lake City: Deseret Book Co., 2009], 95). To be a purer vessel in receiving revelation, begin the repentance process before supplicating the Lord. "And if ye are purified and cleansed from all sin, ye shall ask whatsoever you will in the name of Jesus and it shall be done" (D&C 50:29). Elder James E. Talmage echoed this principle, explaining that when praying for a group, personal sanctification becomes important for the whole group: "If you would have your personal prayers reach the Divine destination to which they are addressed, see to it that they are transmitted by a current of pure sincerity, free from the resistance of unrepented sin. Let those who assemble in the sacred circle of united prayer have a care that each is individually clean, lest the supplication be nullified through the obstruction of an offending member" (James E. Talmage, *The Parables of James E. Talmage* [Salt Lake City: Deseret Book Co., 1973], 11–12).

Avoid Counseling God

When we pray, we should avoid telling God what He should do in our lives and how He should do it. Elder Hartman Rector Jr. declared, "To attempt to instruct the Lord in his duties would . . . be out of order" (Hartman Rector Jr., "Our Prayers in Public," in *Prayer*, 69). Often, we think we know what needs to happen in our lives, so we approach the Lord with the attitude that He should grant our specific desires. The prophet Jacob warns against this practice, saying, "Seek not to counsel the Lord, but to take counsel from his hand. For behold, ye yourselves know that he counseleth in wisdom, and in justice, and in great mercy, over all his works" (Jacob 4:10). We sometimes come to the Lord in prayer with strong opinions about how every moment of our lives should transpire. But as we broaden our minds and let go of these prejudices, we open a greater channel for spiritual revelation. "In our search for truth," President Hugh B. Brown counseled, "we must purge ourselves of prejudice, for that closes the mind" (Hugh B. Brown, *The Abundant Life* [Salt Lake City: Deseret Book Co., 1965], 277).

Pray with Your Spouse

Elder Marvin J. Ashton noted, "There is a peculiar daily strength and power that comes to a couple united in prayerful communication to God. I suggest that the marriage partners take turns being voice for each in crying out words of appreciation" (Ashton, "Personal Prayers," 81). Praying with your spouse calls upon God's great power to strengthen your marriage relationship. President Gordon B. Hinckley emphasized the importance of prayer in marriage: "I know of no single practice that will have a more salutary effect upon your lives than the practice of kneeling together as you begin and close each day. Somehow the little storms that seem to afflict every marriage are dissipated when, kneeling before the Lord, you thank him for one another, in the presence of one another, and then together invoke his blessings upon your lives, your home, your loved ones, and your dreams. God then will be your partner, and your daily conversations with him will bring peace into your hearts and a joy into your lives that can come from no other source" (Gordon B. Hinckley, "'Except the Lord Build the House . . . ,'" *Ensign,* June 1971, 71).

Remember to Act

Elder Neal A. Maxwell said, "We sometimes find ourselves praying for others when we should be doing things for them. Prayers are not to be a substitute for service, but a spur thereto" (Maxwell, *Experience,* 97). Likewise, Brigham Young declared, "You know that it is one peculiarity of our faith and religion never to ask the Lord to do a thing without being willing to help him all that we are able; and then the Lord will do the rest" (Young, *Discourses,* 43). By doing good works in addition to prayer, we call upon the powers of Heaven to bless us. "Yea, he that repenteth and exerciseth faith, and bringeth forth good works, and prayeth continually without ceasing—unto such it is given to know the mysteries of God; yea, unto such it shall be given to reveal things which never have been revealed; yea, and it shall be given unto such to bring thousands of souls to repentance, even as it has been given unto us to bring these our brethren to repentance" (Alma 26:22).

Know That the Lord Will Direct Your Path

The Lord takes care of those who follow Him, and He will direct our paths if we will let Him. "And the Lord said unto Enoch: Go forth and do as I have commanded thee, and no man shall pierce thee. Open thy mouth, and it shall be filled, and I will give thee utterance, for all flesh is in my hands, and I will do as seemeth me good" (Moses 6:32). The Lord, knowing all things, has the capacity to unfold our best future. Neal A. Maxwell stated, "God, who knows the beginning from the end, knows, therefore, all that is in between. He could not safely see us through our individual allotments of 'all these things' that shall give us experience if he did not first know 'all things'" (Maxwell, *Experience,* 7). President Spencer W. Kimball testified of God's great love and concern for His children: "And since our Father in Heaven loves us with more love than we have even for ourselves, it means that we can trust in his goodness, we can trust in him; it means that if we continue praying and living as we should, our Father's hand will guide and bless us" (Kimball, "Pray Always," 3).

Pray Over All Things

Elder Marvin J. Ashton stated, "Personal prayers are our own business, and nothing is too unimportant for God" (Ashton, "Personal Prayers," 76). The Lord cares about even our smallest concerns, and He desires to help us in both spiritual and temporal matters. The prophet Alma counseled that the Saints should ask "for whatsoever things ye stand in need, both spiritual and temporal" (Alma 7:23). Likewise, Amulek taught, "Cry unto [God] when ye are in your fields, yea, over all your flocks. Cry unto him in your houses, yea, over all your household, both morning, mid-day, and evening" (Alma 34:20–21). Sometimes we may worry that we weary Heavenly Father with our prayers, or that a particular concern is too menial to trouble Him with. But He is anxious to be a part of our day-to-day lives. Elder Bruce R. McConkie explained, "We are entitled and expected to pray for all things properly needed, whether temporal or spiritual" (McConkie, "Why the Lord Ordained Prayer," 7). President Ezra Taft Benson observed that we must first ask before we can receive: "Sometimes we have not, because we ask not (James 4:2). Think of all the revelations that came to the Prophet Joseph Smith because he was willing to ask the Lord about certain matters and needs" (Benson, *God, Family, Country,* 122).

Pray for Forgiveness

Elder Bruce R. McConkie taught in a sample prayer that seeking forgiveness is necessary to open communication with God. He beseeched, "We confess our sins before thee and seek remission thereof, lest anything stand between us and thee in receiving a free flow of thy Spirit" (Bruce R. McConkie, "Patterns of Prayer," *Ensign,* May 1984, 32). Elsewhere, Elder McConkie asserted, "Prayers are occasions of confession—occasions when in humility and contrition, having broken hearts and contrite spirits, the saints confess their sins to Deity and implore him to grant his cleansing forgiveness." (McConkie, "Why the Lord Ordained Prayer," 7). We confess all our sins to Heavenly Father in prayer, and as we counsel with Him, He will help us to forsake our sins. He will bless us with a greater desire to truly repent and to change our lives for the better. And when our repentance is complete, He will give us the sweet assurance that we have been forgiven. Likewise, when others have wronged us, we can petition the Lord in prayer for the desire and ability to forgive, and for the strength to press forward.

Offer Prayers to Please God, Not Others

President Spencer W. Kimball said, "Difficult as it seems, I have found when praying with others that it is better for our attitude to be concerned with communicating tenderly and honestly with God, rather than worrying over what the listeners may be thinking" (Kimball, "Pray Always," 3). When praying publicly, we must be careful to pray with real intent. Elder Gene R. Cook cautioned, "When we pray publicly, let us be careful to never be swept away in the desire for the honors of men, which might cause us to pray without real intent or to unnecessarily extend the length of our prayers. The same caution applies to those who pray for a mortal audience rather than simply to be heard by the Lord" (Cook, *Answers,* 43–44). Elder Hartman Rector Jr. counseled that as we pray publicly, "The prayer should carefully fit within the time period allotted, and the temptation to preach a sermon while praying should be avoided" (Rector Jr., "Our Prayers in Public," 69). One of the easiest ways for us to avoid these types of prayers is to remember the reason we are praying. We should concentrate on our Heavenly Father, on the purposes of the meeting, and on the unique reasons for gratitude and the special needs of those assembled, and we should simply speak from our hearts.

Pray to Overcome Temptation

Amid great tribulation and persecution against the Church, the Lord taught His Saints to use a powerful shield for protection, "Pray always that you may come off conqueror; yea, that you may conquer Satan, and that you may escape the hands of the servants of Satan that do uphold his work" (D&C 10:5). He also said, "What I say unto one I say unto all; pray always lest that wicked one have power in you, and remove you out of your place" (D&C 93:49). President Joseph Fielding Smith promised, "We may be definitely sure that the Lord will not permit Satan to deceive the earnest seeker after truth when he sincerely prays" (Joseph Fielding Smith, *Answers to Gospel Questions,* 3 vols. [Salt Lake City: Deseret Book Co., 1960], 3:85). George Q. Cannon taught that every temptation can be overcome through prayer: "Prayer is the bulwark of the Saints. It shields and protects those who offer it in sincerity and faith. Without prayer man is exposed to wicked temptations and to every evil. When he goes unto the Lord in humility, he shows Him his weaknesses and the dangers by which he is surrounded. This prompts him who prays to seek unto God for strength to overcome his weaknesses and to resist every temptation" (George Q. Cannon, *Gospel Truth: Discourses and Writings of President George Q. Cannon,* comp. Jerreld L. Newquist [Salt Lake City: Deseret Book Co., 1957], 411).

Pray for Church Leaders

Our Church leaders need—and often ask for—our prayers in their behalf. Joseph F. Smith stated, "There never should be a day pass but all the people composing the Church should lift up their voices in prayer to the Lord to sustain his servants who are placed to preside over them. Not only should they do this in behalf of the president of the stake and his counselors, but they should do it in behalf of the high council, before whom, in connection with the presidency of the stake, matters of vast importance to the members of the Church are brought from time to time for their judgment and counsel. These men should have the faith of their people to sustain them in the discharge of their duties in order that they may be strong in the Lord" (Joseph F. Smith, address given 12 June 1898, Salt Lake Stake, Salt Lake City, Utah). Elder Reed Smoot counseled, "Part of our prayers should be devoted to our leaders: they have great responsibilities. Oh, so many of the people do not realize the responsibilities that fall upon the President and his Counselors these days. It has been so from the beginning and as long as there is life it will continue to be so. Let us pray for our leaders at all times instead of criticizing them, pray that they may be given courage to continue with unflagging zeal from year to year; pray for the power of God to be upon

them" (Reed Smoot, *Conference Report,* Oct. 1940 [Salt Lake City: Deseret Book Co., 2009], 21). Spencer W. Kimball taught that these prayers even offer protection against apostasy: "We pray for the Church leaders. If children all their days in their turn at family prayers and in their secret prayers remember before the Lord the leaders of the Church, they are quite unlikely to ever fall into apostasy. . . . The children who pray for the brethren will grow up loving them, speaking well of them, honoring and emulating them. Those who daily hear the leaders of the Church spoken of in prayer in deep affection will more likely believe the sermons and admonitions they will hear" (Kimball, *Faith,* 202).

Avoid Vain Repetitions

In prayer, we should avoid using contrite words and phrases out of habit or because they sound fitting. "Sincere prayers come from the heart," President James E. Faust taught. "Indeed, sincerity requires that we draw from the earnest feelings of our hearts when we pray rather than using vain repetitions or pretentious affectations" (James E. Faust, "The Lifeline of Prayer," *Ensign*, May 2002, 59). Use words to express what you mean, not to fill up a "proper-sounding" prayer. President Joseph F. Smith counseled, "Let the prayer come from the heart, let it not be in words that are worn into ruts in the beaten tracks of common use, without thought or feeling in the use of those words. Let us speak the simple words, expressing our need, that will appeal most truly to the Giver of every good and perfect gift" (Joseph F. Smith, *Improvement Era*, Aug. 1908, 11:729–32). To the people of ancient America, the Savior taught the same principle: "But when ye pray, use not vain repetitions, as the heathen, for they think that they shall be heard for their much speaking. Be not ye therefore like unto them, for your Father knoweth what things ye have need of before ye ask him" (3 Nephi 13:7–8). We must be vigilant in monitoring our use of repetitive phrases or trite sayings in prayer. Ultimately, the words we speak are not important to God, unless they are used to form the feelings of our hearts.

Dedicate Yourself to God

President John Taylor said, "[Do] you bow in meekness and with sincere desire to seek the blessing of God upon you and your household? That is the way we ought to do, and cultivate a spirit of devotion and trust in God, dedicating ourselves to him, and seeking his blessings" (John Taylor, in *Journal of Discourses,* 21:118). He further declared, "Do not forget to call upon the Lord in your family circles, dedicating yourselves and all you have to God every day of your lives; and seek to do right, and cultivate the spirit of union and love, and the peace and blessing of the Living God will be with us, and he will lead us in the paths of life; and we shall be sustained and upheld by all the holy angels and the ancient patriarchs and men of God, and the veil will become thinner between us and our God, and we will approach nearer to him, and our souls will magnify the Lord of hosts" (Taylor, in *Journal of Discourses,* 20:361). The Lord can make more of our lives than we can. Dedicating what we have to God means giving our all to furthering His work.

Pray for the Lord to Remove Obstacles

When we are working toward righteous goals, the Lord wants to help us accomplish them. We can pray for His help in removing obstacles and working through our problems. President Joseph F. Smith assured, "If we are in trouble, let us go to the Lord and ask him directly and specifically to help us out of the trouble that we are in; and let the prayer come from the heart, let it not be in words that are worn into ruts in the beaten tracks of common use, without thought or feeling in the use of those words. Let us speak the simple words, expressing our need, that will appeal most truly to the Giver of every good and perfect gift" (Smith, *Improvement Era,* 11:729–32). Simple and sincere petitions for the realization of righteous goals are heard of the Lord, and He will respond for our benefit, according to His will. In his "psalm," the prophet Nephi prays, "O Lord, I have trusted in thee, and I will trust in thee forever. . . . Wilt thou make my path straight before me! Wilt thou not place a stumbling block in my way—but that thou wouldst clear my way before me, and hedge not up my way" (2 Nephi 4:33–34).

Study Your Questions and Concerns before Praying about Them

The Lord counseled His Saints, "You have supposed that I would give it unto you, when you took no thought save it was to ask me. But . . . you must study it out in our mind; then you must ask me if it be right" (D&C 9:7–8). In reference to this principle, President Harold B. Lee advised, "Study it out in your mind, get all the knowledge you can by [seeking counsel], and then reach a decision, either an affirmative or negative decision on the matter; then come to your Heavenly Father and ask Him whether your decision is in harmony with His will" (Lee, *Teachings*, 127). It is easy to become discouraged in prayer if we take "no thought save . . . to ask" our Father for counsel (D&C 9:7). But as we reason with Him, make informed decisions, and seek His confirmation, we will eventually receive the divine direction we seek.

Offer Prayers of Only Thanksgiving and Adoration

Robert L. Millet taught, "One practice that I have found particularly meaningful—especially when I find myself reciting words instead of communing with God—is to devote myself to a prayer in which I ask the Lord for absolutely nothing but instead express sincere gratitude for all my blessings. This kind of prayer pays remarkable dividends and settles the soul like few other efforts" (Robert L. Millet, *Gospel Scholar Series: Selected Writings of Robert L. Millet* [Salt Lake City: Deseret Book Co., 2000], 434). Similarly, President Ezra Taft Benson counseled, "The Prophet Joseph is reported to have said at one time that one of the greatest sins of which the Latter-day Saints would be guilty is the sin of ingratitude. I presume most of us have not thought of that as a great sin. There is a great tendency for us in our prayers—and in our pleadings with the Lord—to ask for additional blessings. Sometimes I feel we need to devote more of our prayers to expressions of gratitude and thanksgiving for blessings already received" (Ezra Taft Benson, "Receive All Things with Thankfulness," *New Era,* Nov. 1976, 4). By offering prayers full only of thanks, we witness to the Lord our gratitude. We also show Him that we will go to Him without being prompted by our needs or concerns. "And he who receiveth all things with thankfulness shall be made glorious; and the things

of this earth shall be added unto him, even an hundred fold, yea, more" (D&C 78:19). Elder Joseph B. Wirthlin gave suggestions for offering prayers of thanks: "Meditate for a while on the things for which you really are grateful. Look for them. They don't have to be grand or glorious. Sometimes we should express our gratitude for the small and simple things like the scent of the rain, the taste of your favorite macaroni and cheese recipe, or the sound of a loved one's voice" (Joseph B. Wirthlin, "Improving Our Prayers," address given 21 Jan. 2003 at Brigham Young University, *Brigham Young University 2002–2003 Speeches* [Provo, UT: Brigham Young University, 2004]). In addition to prayers of gratitude, we need to offer prayers of love and worship. Elder Neal A. Maxwell stated, "Some prayers ought to be prayers of sheer adoration. Adoration, absent of any petition, even occasionally would be a better mix than prayers that are perpetual petitions and relentless requests, minus adoration and appreciation" (Maxwell, "What Should We Pray For?" in *Prayer,* 49).

Be Attentive and Alert while Praying

"The trouble with most of our prayers," President Gordon B. Hinckley declared, "is that we give them as if we were picking up the telephone and ordering groceries—we place our order and hang up. We need to meditate, contemplate, think of what we are praying about and for and then speak to the Lord as one man speaketh to another" (Hinckley, Smithfield/Logan Utah Regional Conference). When we concentrate on our petition and focus on the importance of what we are doing, the Lord will bless us. As the prophet Jacob taught, "I, Jacob, would speak unto you that are pure in heart. Look unto God with firmness of mind, and pray unto him with exceeding faith, and he will console you in your afflictions, and he will plead your cause, and send down justice upon those who seek your destruction" (Jacob 3:1). Sincere and meaningful prayer requires a clear and alert mind. Elder Neal A. Maxwell taught, "Fatigue tends to produce prayers that are hasty generalities. This suggests that to pray only just before retirement at the end of a taxing day is to adversely affect the content of our prayers" (Maxwell, "What Should We Pray For?" 51). Robert L. Millet noted, "Fatigue also makes it extremely difficult to enjoy our prayers. . . . It may be worthwhile occasionally to have prayer well before going to bed while our mind and body are in a position to do more than utter a few well-worn but familiar phrases" (Millet, *Selected Writings,* 434).

In Public Prayer, Speak for the Group

When praying publicly, be sure to use the pronoun "we," as in "We thank thee for" or "We say these things in the name of." President Ezra Taft Benson explained, "Our public prayers need not be everlasting to be immortal. We are advised not to multiply many words (3 Nephi 19:24) and to avoid vain repetitions (Matthew 6:7). An invocation should set the spiritual tone of the meeting, and the benediction should leave the people on a high spiritual plane, because they have been present when one has talked with God. It is the feeling rather than the length which determines a good public prayer" (Benson, *God, Family, Country*, 125). Elder Hartman Rector Jr. declared, "In content [public] prayer should be directed to the Lord and not used to impress listeners as rhetoric . . . . Public prayer should express the gratitude, needs, desires—even fears—of the whole associated group. . . . The prayer should predominantly be an expression of thanks and a plea for help from God" (Rector Jr., "Our Prayers in Public," 70).

Pray for Family Members

"We pray for our own family members, their incomings and outgoings, their travels, their work, and all pertaining to them," President Spencer W. Kimball explained. "When children pray audibly for their brothers and sisters, it is likely that quarreling and conflicts and jarrings will be lessened" (Kimball, *Faith,* 203). Praying for family members helps us build a greater appreciation for them. President N. Eldon Tanner counseled, "If children pray for their parents, it makes them more appreciative of their parents, and as they pray for one another, they feel closer to one another and part of each other, especially as they realize that they are talking to their Father in Heaven while on their knees in family or secret prayer. Then is when we forget our differences and think of the best in others, and pray for their well-being and for strength to overcome our own weaknesses" (N. Eldon Tanner, *Conference Report,* Oct. 1967 [Salt Lake City: Deseret Book Co., 2009], 55–56). Children who pray for their parents learn to respect them more and are better able to follow the commandment to "honor thy father and thy mother" (1 Nephi 17:55). Similarly, parents are commanded to pray for their children: "Pray in your families unto the Father, always in my name, that . . . your children may be blessed" (3 Nephi 18:21)

Take Time to Listen during Prayer

Be patient during your prayers and let there be moments of silence; the Lord may be waiting to respond. Elder Gene R. Cook taught, "Since the Lord usually speaks in a still, small voice, we often won't hear his answers unless we take the time to listen. I believe the best prayers are often filled with spaces of silence—we're not only talking to our Father, but we're also listening to his responses. Then, when the prayer is over, we can continue to seek feelings and answers by remaining on our knees for a few moments before we move on with the concerns of the day" (Cook, *Answers,* 48). Likewise, Bishop H. Burke Peterson stated, "Listening is an essential part of praying. Answers from the Lord come quietly—ever so quietly. In fact, few hear his answers audibly with their ears. We must be listening carefully or we will never recognize them. Most answers from the Lord are felt in our heart as a warm comfortable expression, or they may come as thoughts to our mind. They come to those who are prepared and who are patient" (H. Burke Peterson, "Adversity and Prayer," *Ensign,* Jan. 1974, 18).

Remember That the Lord Is on Your Side

Elder Richard L. Evans exhorted, "Our Father in heaven is not an umpire who is trying to count us out. He is not a competitor who is trying to outsmart us. He is not a prosecutor who is trying to convict us. He is a Loving Father who wants our happiness and eternal progress and everlasting opportunity and glorious accomplishment, and who will help us all he can if we will but give him, in our lives, the opportunity to do so with obedience and humility and faith and patience" (Richard L. Evans, *Conference Report,* Oct. 1956 [Salt Lake City: Deseret Book Co., 2009], 101). When we see our Father in Heaven as wanting to bless rather than punish us, we can open up and share with Him all the feelings of our hearts. Neal A. Maxwell explained, "'Hold on,' 'fear not'—these are the words of Him who has passed perfectly through 'all these things,' and who now seeks to bring us lovingly and safely through our own individually designed experiences" (Maxwell, *Experience,* 5).

Use "Amen" with Meaning

Rather than simply a word we use to end a prayer, the term "Amen" has great significance. Elder Carlos E. Asay stated, "This word is used to express solemn ratification, acceptance, or hearty approval. When a person says 'Amen' at the end of a prayer, he binds himself, in a sense, to the words spoken" (Carlos E. Asay, "The Language and Pattern of Prayer," in *Prayer,* 37). Elder Asay also reminds us that for public prayers, "the speaker's 'Amen' is a signal for all to give an audible response. This combined 'Amen' shows that the members of the group agree with the prayer and are party to what has been pronounced" (Ibid). We should not say "Amen" as a formality of vain repetition. Whether in a personal or a public prayer, we should be grateful for the chance to express our appreciation and approval.

Follow the Spirit to Know What to Ask For

"He that asketh in the Spirit asketh according to the will of God; wherefore it is done even as he asketh" (D&C 46:30). Listening to the Spirit's guidance is essential if we are to ask according to God's will, for "we know not what we should pray for as we ought: but the Spirit itself maketh intercession for us" (Romans 8:26). President Spencer W. Kimball taught, "The Holy Ghost is a revelator. . . . He is an inspirer and will put words in our mouths, enlighten our understandings and direct our thoughts" (Kimball, *Teachings,* 23). Elder Neal A. Maxwell testified, "God sees things as they really are and as they will become. We don't! In order to tap that precious perspective during our prayers, we must rely upon the promptings of the Holy Ghost. With access to that kind of knowledge, we would then pray for what we and others should have—*really* have. With the Spirit prompting us, we will not ask 'amiss'" (Maxwell, "What Should We Pray For?" 45). It would be hard to overemphasize the importance of this critical insight. When we allow ourselves to be prompted in our prayers, we can receive instruction, understanding, and even answers in the very act of praying.

Incorporate Childlike Qualities when Praying

The Lord Himself declared, "Except ye be converted and become as little children, ye shall not enter into the kingdom of heaven" (Matthew 18:3). Elder Marvin J. Ashton said that when he is moved by the prayers of small children, he is "reminded that perhaps our prayers cannot enter the kingdom of God unless they are childlike in faith, humility, and purpose. Children seem to have a very personal way of talking to God. They speak to him without fear as a friend. Yes, they seem to speak to him as if he were right there with them. Their words are powerful in directness and simplicity" (Ashton, "Personal Prayers," 74). Let your prayers be simple focusing your energy into your desires and petitions and, most importantly, your faith. "When a little child bows down in its perfect simplicity and asks the Father for a blessing," President Joseph F. Smith said, "the Father hears the voice, and will answer in blessings upon his head, because the child is innocent and asks in full trust and confidence. These are simple principles that I have sought to impress upon your minds. They are simple, but necessary, and essential" (Joseph F. Smith, address given 25 Nov. 1917 at Granite Stake Conference, Salt Lake City, Utah).

Pray for Comfort and Peace

We are commanded to seek Heavenly Father if we are sad or in distress. In the Doctrine and Covenants, the Savior instructed, "If thou art sorrowful, call on the Lord thy God with supplication, that your souls may be joyful" (136:29). Knowing that we can go to our Heavenly Father for comfort is one of our greatest blessings. President David O. McKay said, "A belief in God brings peace to the soul. An assurance that God is our Father, into whose presence we can go for comfort and guidance, is a never-failing source of comfort" (McKay, *Happiness, 226*). Praying for and receiving comfort from a loving Father helps us develop a stronger relationship with Him. As God manifests His love in this way, we can witness and show gratitude for His ever-present care and concern for our welfare.

Pray in Solitude

Jesus taught, "But thou, when thou prayest, enter into thy closet, and when thou hast shut thy door, pray to thy Father which is in secret; and thy Father which seeth in secret shall reward thee openly" (Matthew 6:6). President Spencer W. Kimball likewise taught of the importance of solitude in prayer: "Solitude is rich and profitable. When we pray alone with God, we shed all sham and pretense, all hypocrisy and arrogance. The Savior found His mountains and slipped away to pray. Paul, the great apostle, could not seem to get into the spirit of his new calling until he had found cleansing solitude down in Arabia: for purification; for repentance; for forgiveness, to break the seal of worldly covering, to shed his film, his skintight suit of worldliness. He went into solitude a worldly man and came out cleansed, prepared, regenerated" (Spencer W. Kimball, address given 11 Oct. 1961 at Brigham Young University, BYU Speeches of the Year, 1961 [Salt Lake City: Deseret Book Co., 2009], 10). In a similar way, we can find particular focus in our prayers if we will take the time to find a secluded place where we can be alone as we approach our Heavenly Father's throne. This is particularly true when we pray out loud.

Accompany Prayer with Fasting

One of the most important ways to increase the power and effectiveness of our prayers is to fast. As members of the Church, we fast the first Sunday of every month and contribute what we would have spent on food as a fast offering to the poor. But we can fast anytime that we need special guidance or direction from Heaven. At a priesthood leadership meeting, Ezra Taft Benson remarked, "I am confident that as leaders we do not do enough fasting and praying. If you want to get the spirit . . . try fasting for a period. I don't mean just missing one meal, then eat twice as much the next meal. I mean really fasting, and praying during that period. It will do more to give you the real spirit of your office and calling and permit the Spirit to operate through you than anything I know" (Ezra Taft Benson, address given 13 Sept. 1952 in Fresno, California). Whether we have a leadership position in the Church or are just seeking more effective communication with our Father in Heaven, the Lord has promised that when we fast and pray, He will answer, "Here I am" (see Isaiah 58:9). President Joseph F. Smith also taught that we must fast and pray with real intent, "A man may fast and pray till he kills himself; and there isn't any necessity for it; nor wisdom in it. I say to my brethren, when they are fasting, and praying for the sick, and for those who need faith and prayer,

do not go beyond what is wise and prudent in fasting and prayer. The Lord can hear a simple prayer offered in faith, in half a dozen words, and he will recognize fasting that may not continue more than twenty-four hours, just as readily and effectually as he will answer a prayer of a thousand words and fasting for a month" (Joseph F. Smith, *Conference Report,* Oct. 1912 [Salt Lake City: Deseret Book Co., 2009], 133–34). King Benjamin taught, "And see that all these things are done in wisdom and order; for it is not requisite that a man should run faster than he has strength" (Mosiah 4:27).

Accept God's Answers with Gratitude and a Willing Heart

In order to accept Heavenly Father's will, we need to ready our hearts to hear it. The Lord said, "Therefore, prepare thy heart to receive and obey the instructions which I am about to give unto you; for all those who have this law revealed unto them must obey the same" (D&C 132:3). The Lord commands us to thank Him for our blessings, and these blessing include His answers to our petitions—even when the answers are not what we expected or wanted. "The Lord requireth the heart and a willing mind" (D&C 64:34). Part of accepting the Lord's will is to follow His counsel for us, whatever it may be. President Spencer W. Kimball taught, "How should we pray? We should pray in faith, but with awareness that when the Lord answers it may not be with the answer we expect or desire. Our faith must be that God's choice for us is right" (Kimball, *Faith,* 207). The Lord himself declared: "Ye are commanded in all things to ask of God, who giveth liberally; and that which the Spirit testifies unto you even so I would that ye should do in all holiness of heart, walking uprightly before me, considering the end of your salvation, doing all things with prayer and thanksgiving" (D&C 46:7).

Recognize What It Means to Pray in the Name of Jesus Christ

In prayer, we supplicate our Father in Heaven and seal that supplication in the name of Jesus Christ. President Joseph F. Smith explained, "We . . . accept without any question the doctrines we have been taught by the Prophet Joseph Smith and by the Son of God himself, that we pray to God, the Eternal Father, in the name of his only begotten Son, to whom also our father Adam and his posterity have prayed from the beginning" (Joseph F. Smith, *Conference Report,* Oct. 1916 [Salt Lake City: Deseret Book Co., 2009], 6). Praying in Christ's name seals our prayer and consecrates our performance unto Him. We read in 2 Nephi 32:9, "But behold, I say unto you that ye must pray always, and not faint; that ye must not perform any thing unto the Lord save in the first place ye shall pray unto the Father in the name of Christ, that he will consecrate thy performance unto thee." Praying in Christ's name means aligning our wills with his. "We pray in Christ's name when our mind is the mind of Christ, and our wishes the wishes of Christ—when his words abide in us" (John 15:7). We then ask for things it is possible for God to grant. Many prayers remain unanswered because they are not in Christ's name at all; they in no way represent his mind, but spring out of the selfishness of man's heart" (Bible Dictionary, "Prayer," 753).

Address Heavenly Father with Respect

Following the Savior's example, we should always use the words "Thee," "Thou," "Thy," and "Thine" when addressing God the Father. In this manner, we differentiate our everyday language from that which we speak in supplication to God. Spencer W. Kimball stated, "In all our prayers, it is well to use the pronouns *thee, thou, thy,* and *thine* instead of *you, your,* and *yours,* inasmuch as they have come to indicate respect" (Kimball, *Faith,* 201). Using these reverential pronouns helps us maintain a humble, worshipful attitude during prayer, and shows Heavenly Father our willingness to submit to Him and to His will.

Pray with Others

Our petitions to Heavenly Father can be more effective when we unite our prayers with those of other believers. "To be unified in prayer brings more strength," stated Elder Gene R. Cook. "If you can get a number of people praying for you—a family, your brothers and sisters, friends, ward members—the unity in strength that results will help to bring increased power to your request" (Cook, *Answers,* 68). The Lord has always commanded His Saints to pray together. "And the church did meet together oft, to fast and to pray, and to speak one with another concerning the welfare of their souls" (Moroni 6:5). He also taught of the power of a united prayer: "Whatsoever ye shall ask in faith, being united in prayer according to my command, ye shall receive" (D&C 29:6). From time to time, members of the Church are asked to unite in fasting and prayer on behalf of the victims of natural disasters, or on behalf of others in need. Bishops, on occasion, may ask ward members to unite in prayer for the sick or otherwise afflicted. And families are wise to unite in prayer for each other. When we combine our prayers, we call down blessings from heaven.

After Receiving an Answer from God, Write it Down

Throughout the scriptures, the Lord directs His people to record the things He reveals to them. For example, He commanded Moses, "Behold, I reveal unto you concerning this heaven, and this earth; write the words which I speak" (Moses 2:1). When the Lord gives you an answer through His appointed means, it is critical that you recall and apply these teachings and instructions in your life. Look back to these records often to review how you have grown and progressed and to remind yourself of the Lord's love and concern for you. Remember that as you receive inspiration from on High and write it down, you are recording your own personal scripture!

Make Prayer an Anchor in Your Life

"All through my life," reflected President Ezra Taft Benson, "the counsel to depend on prayer has been prized above almost any other advice I have ever received. It has become an integral part of me, an anchor, a constant source of strength, and the basis of my knowledge of things divine" (Ezra Taft Benson, "Improving Communication with our Heavenly Father," in *Prayer,* 110). Use prayer through all the trials and challenges you face. Make prayer an anchor so that when you are faced with a trial, your thoughts go immediately to prayer and to the comfort and guidance of the Lord. Bishop H. Burke Peterson declared that "Our Father in heaven . . . is the key to our enjoying sweetness in adversity—in gaining strength from our trials—he and he alone. . . . The best way I know to keep close to the source of this great strength is through prayer. . . . As we learn to develop this two-way communication, the standard of our life will improve. We will see things more clearly; we will try harder to do better; we will see the real joy that can come through trials and testing. Although problems will still be with us, peace, contentment, and true happiness will be ours in abundance" (H. Burke Peterson, "Adversity and Prayer," *Prayer*, 107).

Do Not Attempt to Force Answers

Do not try to force answers to your prayers. "The Spirit is sensitive and cannot be subjected to constraint, control, and compulsion," stated Elder L. Lionel Kendrick. "It is independent and responds only to invitations and not to impositions" (L. Lionel Kendrick, "Personal Revelation," *Ensign,* Sept. 1999, 7). When you ask Heavenly Father a specific question, know that the timing of His response will be according to His knowledge of all things—past, present, and future. Often, this means that you must wait patiently to receive the inspiration you seek. Likewise, Elder Gerald L. Lund counseled, "The timing of revelation or answers to prayers is . . . completely determined by the Lord. We can do things that enhance our readiness to receive revelation. We can facilitate things so revelation comes more quickly than it might otherwise. But when it comes is still the Lord's decision. We may *influence* the timing, but we cannot *determine* it" (Gerald L. Lund, *Hearing the Voice of the Lord: Principles and Patterns of Personal Revelation* [Salt Lake City: Deseret Book, 2007]). Clearly, the Spirit will not speak to us until we are ready. Trying to force inspiration may even lead us to receive false direction from the adversary.

Picture Heavenly Father as You Pray

If you picture Heavenly Father in your mind as you pray, you can feel more reverence and awe—and feel closer to Him. The Lord promised: "I am in your midst, but you do not see me. The Holy Ghost bears the sure witness. Mine eyes are upon you. The day cometh when ye shall know that I am" (D&C 38:7–8). Sister Patricia T. Holland asked, "Do we really picture an actual father when we pray? Do we think of Him—do we *truly* think of Him—as our Father? Do we spend any time on our knees trying to picture the being to whom we pray?" (Holland and Holland, *Heaven*, 37). President David O. McKay similarly asked, "When you kneel down to pray at night, do you feel his nearness, his personality hearing you, do you feel a power that operates perhaps as the radio or a greater power so that you feel that you are communing with him?" (David O. McKay, *Conference Report*, Oct. 1954 [Salt Lake City: Deseret Book Co., 2009], 84). To keep our focus on our Heavenly Father when we pray, we should seek to see with our spiritual eyes and hear with our spiritual ears.

Make It a Habit to Pray Two or Three Times a Day

Our lives can get hectic, and it often seems that we don't have time for one more thing. But whatever else we accomplish during our waking hours, let us not forget to pray regularly to our Heavenly Father. President Joseph F. Smith counseled, "[Observe] that great commandment given of the Master, always to remember the Lord, to pray in the morning, and in the evening, and always remember to thank him for blessings that you receive day by day. . . . It is the commandment of the Lord that we shall remember God morning and evening, and as the Book of Mormon tells us, 'at all times'" (Smith, *Conference Report,* Oct. 1914, 6). It is important to make consistent daily prayers a habit, so that even when we are busy, we automatically get on our knees. Elder John A. Widtsoe declared, "No prayer is unheard. The place and time of prayer are of less importance. Morning, noon and night, prayer is always fitting. However, it is well to be orderly, and to beget habits of prayer, and certain hours of the day should therefore be set aside for prayer, both in private and in the family" (John A. Widtsoe, *Rational Theology* [Salt Lake City: Deseret Book Co., 1915], 76–77).

Be Prepared for Increased Opposition from the Adversary

As you increase the frequency and intensity of your prayers, the adversary will increase his efforts to lead you away from the Lord. Gene R. Cook warned, "I've found that when you begin to pray for something that really matters, many times things get worse, not better. Often the cause is Satan and his helpers, who are doing their best to make sure you don't succeed" (Cook, *Answers,* 137). Elder Cook also explained, "When we're seeking answers to prayers, the Lord will surely test us. He wants us to see if we will serve and love him at any cost. He wants us to see if we will continue in faith even if we don't receive the answer we had hoped for" (Ibid). The prophet Ether taught, "Ye receive no witness until after the trial of your faith" (Ether 12:6). Yet we know that as we obey Him and put our trust in Him, the Lord will bless us to withstand the temptations we face. Ezra Taft Benson pointed Saints toward hope in the face of trials: "There may come persecution; there may come opposition . . . But if we place our trust in the Almighty and do that which is right, there will come an inner assurance, an inner calm, a peace that will bring joy and happiness to our souls" (Ezra Taft Benson, *Conference Report,* Apr. 1954 [Salt Lake City: Deseret Book Co., 2009], 59).

Pray More Earnestly when the Need Warrants

Greater needs call for greater pleading. Elder Bruce R. McConkie taught, "Now here is a marvelous thing. Note it well. The Son of God 'prayed more earnestly' [see Luke 22:45]! He who did all things well, whose every word was right, whose every emphasis was proper; he to whom the Father gave his Spirit without measure . . . 'prayed more earnestly,' teaching us . . . that all prayers, his included, are not alike, and that a greater need calls forth more earnest and faith-filled pleadings before the throne of him to whom the prayers of the saints are a sweet savor" (Bruce R. McConkie, "Why the Lord Ordained Prayer," 8). As Robert L. Millet expounded, "Indeed, some thorns in the flesh call forth prayers of great intensity (see 2 Corinthians 12:7–10), supplications and pleading that are certainly out of the ordinary. Such vexations of the soul are not typical, not part of our daily prayer life. Just as it would be a mistake to suppose that Jacob or Enos wrestled with God in prayer every day, so you and I are not expected to involve ourselves with the same tenacity, to be involved in the same bending of the soul on a regular basis. But now and then in the eternal scheme of things, we must pass through the fire in order to come through life purified and refined and thus prepared to dwell one day in everlasting burnings with God and Christ and holy beings" (Millet, *Selected Writings,* 438–39).

Remember Your Divine Nature

We feel a sense of importance when we realize our place in the universe—when we know where we came from and where we are going. Concerning prayer, Elder John A. Widtsoe taught, "A man never finds perfect peace, never reaches afar unless he penetrates to some degree the unseen world, and reaches out to touch the hands, as it were, of those who live in that unseen world, the world out of which we came, the world into which we shall go" (John A. Widstoe, *Conference Report,* Oct. 1938 [Salt Lake City: Deseret Book Co., 2009], 128). Each of us has infinite worth and is entitled to commune with and receive direction from the Creator of us all. "As soon as we learn the true relationship in which we stand toward God (namely, God is our Father, and we are his children), then at once prayer becomes natural and instinctive on our part (Matt. 7:7–11). Many of the so-called difficulties about prayer arise from forgetting this relationship" (Bible Dictionary, "Prayer," 752). When we remember who we are, and who our Father is, we will not forget to pray—often and sincerely.

Wait Patiently on the Lord

One thing we could all use more of is patience, and waiting on the Lord is particularly important. Elder Joseph B. Wirthlin said, "Sometimes the hardest thing we can do is wait. The Lord has his own timetable, and although it may frustrate us, his timing is always perfect. When we rest in the Lord, we allow Him to work His will for us in His own time and in His own way . . . Instead of worrying or grumbling that our prayers have gone unanswered, we should delight ourselves in the Lord. Be grateful. Be happy. Know that the Lord, in His time, will bring about all your righteous desires—sometimes in ways we predict, others in ways we could not have possibly foreseen. What a wonderful recipe for happiness and peace" (Joseph B. Wirthlin, *Press On* [Salt Lake City: Deseret Book Co., 2007). Though perhaps not when we expect, answers do come. And when we wait patiently on the Lord, we will find greater peace in our lives. President David O. McKay noted, "It is true that the answers to our prayers may not always come as direct and at the time, nor in the manner, we anticipate; but they do come, and at a time and in a manner best for the interests of him who offers the supplication" (David O. McKay, *Conference Report*, Apr. 1969 [Salt Lake City: Deseret Book Co., 2009], 152–53). The Lord will grant peace to those who wait with faith. Elder Rex D. Pinegar

said, "Sometimes, when our prayers are not answered as we desire, we may feel the Lord has rejected us or that our prayer was in vain. We may begin to doubt our worthiness before God, or even the reality and power of prayer. That is when we must continue to pray with patience and faith and to listen for that peace" (Rex D. Pinegar, "Peace through Prayer," in *Peace* [Salt Lake City: Deseret Book, 1998], 75).

Pray while Driving

If you are alone in your car, turn off the radio and other distractions and take time to speak with and listen to the Lord. Obviously, if you are driving, you can't kneel, close your eyes, or bow your head, but your can still use the time for meditation and conversation with the Lord. Many of us spend a significant amount of time in our cars, and it is easy to fill that time with music or news on the radio. We can forget what a luxury it is in our busy lives to have uninterrupted time alone. By using these moments to check in with our Heavenly Father, we will find it easier to keep a prayer in our heart.

Share Your Feelings and Concerns with Heavenly Father

The Lord has commanded us, "In every thing by prayer and supplication with thanksgiving let your requests be made known unto God" (Philippians 4:6). Let your prayers be full, filled with all your thoughts and feelings, and all your worries and concerns. Speaking of praying privately, President Spencer W. Kimball taught, "If in these special moments of prayer we hold back from the Lord, it may mean that some blessings may be withheld from us. After all, we pray as petitioners before an all-wise Heavenly Father, so why should we ever think to hold back feelings or thoughts which bear upon our needs and our blessings? We hope that our people will have very bounteous prayers" (Kimball, *Teachings,* 125). Next time you pray, think about making it a "bounteous prayer."

Don't Go another Day without Praying!

President Joseph F. Smith counseled, "What shall we do if we have neglected our prayers? Let us begin to pray. If we have neglected any other duty, let us seek unto the Lord for his Spirit, that we may know wherein we have erred and lost our opportunities, or let them pass by us unimproved" (Smith, in *Journal of Discourses* [Salt Lake City: Deseret Book Co., 1877], 18:91). Often we may neglect prayer, sometimes by letting too much time lapse between prayers, and sometimes by not praying sincerely or attentively. But our Heavenly Father is quick to welcome us back; in fact, He has repeatedly *commanded* us to return to Him. Elder Gene R. Cook instructed, "If you are not in the habit, it is time to get in the habit. . . . If you don't believe prayer will work, it is time to put it to the test anew. I promise you that if you will follow the Lord and seek him with all your heart, he will surely bless you—and he will surely give you answers to your prayers" (Cook, *Answers,* 101).

Pray for Increased Spirituality and for Strength to Overcome Weaknesses

Elder Marvin J. Ashton noted, "There are strength and power and discipline rewards in communicating with God on a continuing personal and private basis" (Marvin J. Ashton, "Know He Is There," address given 10 Nov. 1992 at Brigham Young University, in *Brigham Young University 1992–93 Speeches* [Provo, UT: Brigham Young University, 1993]). We can increase our inner strength and peace through prayer. "If I could wish for anyone a priceless gift," Ezra Taft Benson reflected, "it would not be wealth, profound wisdom, or the honors of men. I would rather pass on the key to inner strength and security which my father gave to me when he advised, 'Receive His aid through prayer'" (Benson, *God, Family, Country,* 112). George Q. Cannon taught that we can overcome our weaknesses through prayer: "Every defect in human character can be corrected through the exercise of faith and pleading with the Lord for the gifts that He has said He will give unto those who believe and obey His commandments" (George Q. Cannon, *Juvenile Instructor,* 1 Oct. 1896, 31:572).

Pray in the Same Place

Hallowing a special place for prayer, and then praying there regularly, can help ready our hearts for personal revelation. Robert L. Millet said, "One of the things most needed in our prayer lives is consistency and regularity. Some people find it helpful to pray often in the same place. One man I know set aside a special place in his home, a place which over the years came to be like unto a personal sacred grove. It seemed when he entered that room that he felt a hallowed presence. In fact, that is exactly what had happened over the years; because some of the most profound insights and some of the sweetest feelings and impressions had come to him in that room, it had come to represent almost a holy of holies within his home, which was his temple" (Millet, *Selected Writings,* 436–37). As an added benefit, if we have set aside a specific place for prayer, that place itself can serve as a reminder to pray.

Pray for the Companionship of the Holy Ghost

"What do you pray for?" President Joseph F. Smith asked. He then answered, "You pray that God may recognize you, that he may hear your prayers, and that he may bless you with his Spirit, and that he may lead you into all truth and show you the right way; that he will warn you against wrong and guide you into the right path; that you may not fall astray, that you may not veer into the wrong way unto death, but that you may keep in the narrow way" (Smith, *Doctrine,* 215). Praying for the companionship of the Spirit of God is one of our greatest privileges. We can pray for the ever-guiding hand of a loving and omniscient Father. "Whenever you are in doubt about any duty or work which you have to perform," President Wilford Woodruff counseled, "never proceed to do anything until you go and labour in prayer and get the Holy Spirit. Wherever the Spirit dictates you to go or to do, that will be right; and, by following its dictates, you will come out right" (Wilford Woodruff, in *Journal of Discourses* [Salt Lake City: Deseret Book Co., 2009], 5:85).

Give to the Poor and Needy

The blessings we receive from our Heavenly Father are innumerable. In return, we are commanded to give of our substance to others. King Benjamin taught, "And now, if God, who has created you, on whom you are dependent for your lives and for all that ye have and are, doth grant unto you whatsoever ye ask that is right, in faith, believing that ye shall receive, O then, how ye ought to impart of the substance that ye have one to another" (Mosiah 4:21). Amulek explained that answers to prayer are contingent upon our care of those who are less fortunate: "If ye turn away the needy, and the naked, and visit not the sick and afflicted, and impart of your substance, if ye have, to those who stand in need—I say unto you, if ye do not any of these things, behold, your prayer is in vain, and availeth you nothing" (Alma 34:28). When we give to the poor, we witness to the Lord our faithfulness and gratitude towards Him. We can also catch a glimpse of the love the Savior has for those we serve. And as we show our loyalty and sincerity by giving to others, Heavenly Father will be quicker to hear and answer our prayers.

Keep the Commandments

"He that keepeth [God's] commandments receiveth truth and light, until he is glorified in truth and knoweth all things" (D&C 93:28). We are able to receive answers from the Lord when we have prepared ourselves by following His commandments. President Harold B. Lee warned that not keeping the commandments can lead us to deception: "We get our answers from the source of the power we list to obey. If we're following the ways of the devil, we'll get answers from the devil. If we're keeping the commandments of God, we'll get our answers from God" (Harold B. Lee, *Stand Ye in Holy Places* [Salt Lake City: 1974], 137–38). Our personal righteousness is the key that opens the door to truth and light. As the Lord Himself counseled, "If ye will not harden your hearts, and ask me in faith, believing that ye shall receive, with diligence in keeping my commandments, surely these things shall be made known unto you" (1 Nephi 15:7–11).

Pray in the Temple

In the sanctity of the Lord's house, we can prepare our hearts and minds to commune with God and receive personal revelation. President Ezra Taft Benson taught, "In the peace of these lovely temples, sometimes we find solutions to the serious problems of life. Under the influence of the Spirit, sometimes pure knowledge flows to us there. Temples are places of personal revelation. When I have been weighed down by a problem or a difficulty, I have gone to the house of the Lord with a prayer in my heart for answers. These answers have come in clear and unmistakable ways" (Ezra Taft Benson, *The Teachings of Ezra Taft Benson* [Salt Lake City: Deseret Book Co, 1988], 251). If we are blessed to live in proximity to a temple, we can go there in prayer, knowing that there is nowhere on earth that is closer to Heaven. We should go to the temple often and prayerfully seek answers to the questions in our lives.

Pray for a Predetermined Length of Time

Set aside a predetermined amount of time for personal prayer, perhaps 30 or 45 minutes. Although it seems counterintuitive to let the clock dictate how long a prayer should be, those who have tried this exercise testify that praying for longer than we would normally pray can open up new vistas of insight. Once you have seemingly exhausted the list of things for which you are grateful and the list of concerns you have and blessings you seek, continued prayer and listening can make you more susceptible to the Spirit's promptings. In such moments, the Lord can call to your recollection things that are amiss in your life, or past actions for which you should seek repentance.

Pray for Charity

"But charity is the pure love of Christ, and it endureth forever; and whoso is found possessed of it at the last day, it shall be well with him . . . wherefore . . . pray unto the Father with all the energy of heart, that ye may be filled with this love" (Moroni 7:47–48). As charity is necessary for salvation, it is also a gift from our Heavenly Father and requires sincere prayer for its granting. In the words of Ann Madsen, "I know that we receive the Spirit through prayer and are thus given access to Christlike love. Our lives—mind, body, and spirit—are renewed in this process of sacred communion, and we become like him and like our Father in Heaven who loves and reaches out to each of us" (Ann N. Madsen, "Pray with All Energy of Heart," in *Clothed with Charity: Talks from 1996 Women's Conference* [Salt Lake City: Deseret Book Co., 1997], 107–8).

Hold Hands while Praying as a Family

The moments that a family spends praying together are sacred moments of togetherness. Holding hands while praying symbolizes the unity within the family—each member being connected in a circle. By holding hands during family prayer, your family members can grow closer to one another and come to appreciate the supportive and loving family circle of which they are a part.

Offer a Sacrifice to the Lord

Sacrifice brings forth blessings, and an earnest petition becomes more meaningful when accompanied by sacrifice. "Sacrifice truly can increase the power of our prayers," taught Elder Gene R. Cook, "if we will consecrate that sacrifice to the Lord. Suppose, for example, you are a mother or father with a son who is straying from the path of righteousness. I believe you can do much to pray him home. You can do much to fast him home. You can repent enough of your own sins that, through your sacrifice, the Lord may intervene more in his life and save the boy. It's not that you're paying for your own sins—Jesus did that. But through your agency, through your sacrifice, you are able to receive blessings that you otherwise would not be able to obtain" (Cook, *Answers,* 25). In addition to giving up our sins for the Lord, we can give up certain habits in our lives to help us become more spiritual. Perhaps you can sacrifice listening to secular music or watching television for a week. Choose a specific and meaningful sacrifice and consecrate that sacrifice for the earnest petition you are seeking. It will make your plea not only more powerful, but more significant to you.

Don't Postpone Following Heavenly Father's Instructions

We must pray with the intent not only to listen but to obey. Great blessings come from prompt obedience to the Lord's counsel. President Harold B. Lee said, "Now then, all of us should try to strive and give heed to the sudden ideas that come to us, and if we'll give heed to them and cultivate an ear to hear these promptings we too—each of us—can grow in the spirit of revelation" (Lee, *Teachings,* 416). He further declared, "Let the Holy Spirit's promptings guide you night and day, fill your soul with love and guard you from harm, protect you from evil and make you keenly sensitive to the impressions of the Holy Spirit. . . . If you'll learn to give heed to those promptings of the Holy Spirit and then follow them, you'll find those things that are presented to your mind [will come] true very shortly thereafter. If you'll learn to follow your impressions, you'll be amazed to see how you'll walk daily by the spirit of revelation" (Ibid, 242).

Express Gratitude for Your Blessings

"And ye must give thanks unto God in the Spirit for whatsoever blessing ye are blessed with" (D&C 46:32). While expressing gratitude is a commandment from the Lord, it is also a practice that can bring great blessings. As President Spencer W. Kimball assured: "A wonderful and assuring spirit comes over us as we express sincere gratitude to Heavenly Father for our blessings—for the gospel and the knowledge of it that we have been blessed to receive, for the efforts and labors of parents and others in our behalf, for our families and friends, for opportunities, for mind and body and life, for experiences good and helpful throughout our lives, for all of our Father's helps and kindnesses and answered prayers" (Kimball, "Pray Always"). Elder Joseph B. Wirthlin noted, "Thinking of things we are grateful for is a healing balm. It helps us get outside ourselves. It changes our focus from our pains and our trials to the abundance of this beautiful world we live in" (Wirthlin, "Improving Our Prayers").

Pray for Your Enemies

The Lord has commanded, "Love your enemies, do good to them which hate you, Bless them that curse you, and pray for them which despitefully use you" (Luke 6:27–28). Offered with a sincere heart, these prayers have the capacity to bless our lives even more than the lives of those for whom we are praying. Spencer W. Kimball stated, "We pray for our enemies. This will soften our hearts, and perhaps theirs, and we may better seek good in them. And this prayer should not be confined to national enemies but should extend to neighbors, members of the family, and all with whom we have differences" (Kimball, *Faith*, 202). President David O. McKay taught of the power of prayer in removing anger or negative feelings toward others: "I cannot think that a Latter-day Saint will hold enmity in his heart if he will sincerely, in secret, pray God to remove from his heart all feelings of envy and malice toward any of his fellow men" (David O. McKay, *Conference Report*, Oct. 1922, 65). Prayer is our most effective tool against the feelings of anger, bitterness, and hatred that can canker our souls and draw us away from God.

Learn the Language of the Spirit

"There is a way by which persons can keep their consciences clear before God and man," President Lorenzo Snow declared, "and that is to preserve within them the Spirit of God, which is the spirit of revelation to every man and woman. It will reveal to them, even in the simplest of matters, what they shall do, by making suggestions to them. We should try to learn the nature of this spirit, that we may understand its suggestions, and then we will always be able to do right" (Lorenzo Snow, *Conference Report*, Apr. 1899 [Salt Lake City: Deseret Book Co., 2009]). Learning to recognize answers from the Spirit requires practice, study, and effort. Marion G. Romney taught how specific thoughts are often prompted by the Spirit, "Sometimes the Lord puts thoughts in our minds in answer to prayers. . . . [He] gives us peace in our minds" (Marion G. Romney, *Conference Report,* 1975, 7). President Spencer W. Kimball emphasized the peace accompanying answers to prayer: "Learning the language of prayer is a joyous, lifetime experience. Sometimes ideas flood our mind as we listen after our prayers. Sometimes feelings press upon us. A spirit of calmness assures us that all will be well. But always, if we have been honest and earnest, we will experience a good feeling—feeling of warmth for our Father in Heaven and a sense of his love for us. I have felt sorrow because

some of us have not learned the meaning of that calm, spiritual warmth, for it is a witness to us that our prayers have been heard" (Kimball, "Pray Always"). But with all things, learning to recognize the language of the Spirit requires practice and continued effort.

Go into the Wilderness to Pray

God's Spirit powerfully emanates from settings in nature. Being in tune to spiritual thoughts is often easier when we are in the solitude and quiet of God's natural creations. Enos recorded, "Behold, I went to hunt beasts in the forests; and the words which I had often heard my father speak concerning eternal life, and the joy of the saints, sunk deep into my heart" (Enos 1:3). Since ancient times, prophets have ventured into the wilderness or the mountains to commune with God. Enos was in a place where spiritual teachings came more readily to his heart and mind. If you have access to mountains, hiking is a good way to take time to collect and elevate your thoughts as you ascend a mountain. When you have reached a quiet spot to pray, this preparation can do much to increase the power of your experience. The prophet Amulek taught, "But this is not all; ye must pour out your souls in your closets, and your secret places, and in your wilderness" (Alma 34:26).

Accompany Prayer with Priesthood Blessings

Prayers before or after priesthood blessings can bless both the giver and receiver of the blessing. Elder Gene R. Cook taught, "Prayer can help us in many ways when it comes to priesthood blessings. It can help the priesthood brethren know what to say in the blessing so they can speak the will of the Lord. It can help the sick person and his or her family have a witness of the truth of what's been said. It can help them have a feeling of peace and comfort. And it can help everyone involved grow in faith" (Gene R. Cook, Receiving Answers to Our Prayers [Salt Lake City: Deseret Book Co., 1996], 91–92). Prayers before or after blessings are also a way to include concerned family members who may not hold the Melchizedek Priesthood as they add their voice and combine their faith on behalf of a loved one who is ailing.

Pray for Health and Strength

If it is His will, the Lord will grant us not only spiritual strength but physical strength, if we petition Him for it. In the book of Isaiah, we read, "Hast thou not heard, that the everlasting God, the Lord, the Creator of the ends of the earth, fainteth not, neither is weary? . . . He giveth power to the faint; and to them that have no might he increaseth strength. . . . They that wait upon the Lord shall renew their strength; they shall mount up with wings as eagles; they shall run, and not be weary; and they shall walk, and not faint" (40:28–31). When Amulon persecuted the people of Alma in the Book of Mormon, they cried mightily to the Lord. But Amulon "commanded them that they should stop their cries; and he put guards over them to watch them, that whosoever should be found calling on God should be put to death (Mosiah 24:11) . So the people of Alma prayed silently, asking the Lord to ease their burdens. The Lord responded, "Lift up your heads and be of good comfort . . . I will . . . ease the burdens which are put upon your shoulders, that even you cannot feel them upon you backs, even while you are in bondage" (Mosiah 24:13–14). As we humble ourselves and keep the commandments, the Lord will bless us with the strength to carry out His will, if we will but ask.

Thank Heavenly Father for the Gift of His Son

In an address on proper patterns of prayer, Elder Bruce R. McConkie taught that we should thank the Lord "for the blessings of mortal life, and the hope of immortality and eternal life" (McConkie, "Patterns of Prayer"). He also suggested that our prayers include something like "We thank thee for sending the Holy Son Jesus to be the Savior and Redeemer. . . . O how we glory in him and in his blessed name, rejoicing everlastingly that he has ransomed us from temporal and spiritual death; that he is the one Mediator between us and thee; that he has reconciled us unto thee, not imputing unto us our sins, but healing us with his stripes!" (Ibid). In our moments of gratitude to our Father in Heaven, we should not forget the ultimate gift that was given by the Savior, of which we are all beneficiaries. And as we thank Heavenly Fatherf in prayer for the gift of His Son, we can strengthen our appreciation for the Savior and His great Atonement. When we have reverence for His sacrifice, we ready our hearts to commune more purely with the Father.